CHRISTIANS TOGETHER

by Marydel D. and Victor M. Frohne
Illustrated by Eric Von Schmidt

UNITED CHURCH PRESS BOSTON • PHILADELPHIA

The scripture quotations in this publication are, unless otherwise indicated, from the *Revised Standard Version of the Bible*, copyrighted 1946 and 1952 by the Division of Christian Education, National Council of Churches, and used by permission.

Library of Congress Catalog Card Number 64-19470

This book is part of the United Church Curriculum, prepared and published by the Division of Christian Education and the Division of Publication of the United Church Board for Homeland Ministries.

Contents

Dear Boys and Girls:

CHRISTIANS TOGETHER is a book for you to use at home during Lent. In it you will find something to read each day from Ash Wednesday through Easter.

Lent is a time when many Christians feel they want to do something special. They spend more time thinking about Jesus Christ and remembering what he taught us about God's love. They find extra ways to help other people. We hope this book will give you some new ideas about how to celebrate Lent.

There are two ways you can use this book. It can be read with your family when you are all together at your evening meal or just before you go to bed.

Or you can use it by yourself. You can read a part of it each day in your room or in some other place where you can be alone and quiet.

Some days you may choose to read it with your family, and some days you may want to read it by yourself. Whichever you do, you can find something in it to think about each day.

We are Christians together—in the family, in the church school, in the church, with people of other churches, and even with people who lived long ago. As you read this book during the next seven weeks we hope you will find out more about the church and about what it means to be a Christian.

Marydel Frohne
and Victor Frohne

FIRST WEEK

Beginning Lent

First Week | Ash Wednesday

Did you ever wonder how words are made?

Let's take the word *holiday*. Many years ago, the only holidays people had were church holidays such as Christmas and Easter. On these and other church holidays there was no school, no work, and the stores were closed. This was because these were *holy days*, or special days in the life of the church.

Because people looked forward to these holy days as much as we look forward to holidays, they talked a great deal about them. See what happens when you say *holy day* over and over. It sounds like one word, doesn't it? Although it is not spelled the same way, that is how we got our word *holiday*.

Today is a holy day. It is not a holiday too, like Christmas and Easter, but it is an important day in the church. This is Ash Wednesday, the first day of Lent.

Lent is the season that begins today and ends the day before Easter. The season of Lent lasts forty days, not counting Sundays. One reason it is forty days in length is because that is the number of days Jesus spent in the wilderness after his baptism.

Today is called Ash Wednesday because long ago people covered themselves with ashes to show that they were sorry for the wrong things they had done. In some churches the priest or minister will dip his thumb in ashes and make a cross on the foreheads of those who come to church to worship. You may see someone wearing that mark today.

We don't use ashes in this way, but many of our churches hold a special service on each Wednesday during Lent. There may be an Ash Wednesday service tonight in the church that you and your family attend.

Dorothy's Visit

"Mother, Mary Jane wants me to eat supper at her house and sleep there tonight. Oh, please, may I go?" asked Dorothy.

Her mother looked at Mary Jane and asked, "Is it all right with your mother?"

"Yes," answered Mary Jane. "Mother thinks it would be nice for Dorothy to come."

"All right," Dorothy's mother told her, "since it is Friday and there is no school tomorrow, you may go. But you must remember to help with the dishes and to go to sleep early. Don't whisper and giggle all night long!"

"We'll go to bed early," promised Dorothy.

Her mother laughed and said, "Going to bed and going to sleep are two different things." Mary Jane and Dorothy grinned at each other. They knew that was true.

The two girls hurried upstairs to pack Dorothy's suitcase. In went pajamas, slippers, toothbrush, comb, and clean clothes to wear the next day. Both girls took hold of the handle of the suitcase. Swinging it between them, they ran all the way to Mary Jane's house.

After the supper dishes were put away, Mary Jane's mother asked, "Girls, will you please take this cake to Grandma Deller?"

Mary Jane answered with a smile, "Yes, Mother, we'll go right away."

Dorothy followed Mary Jane through the side hedge to the back door of the next house. "Is this where your grandmother lives?" she asked.

"Yes, but Grandma Deller isn't really my grandmother," explained Mary Jane. "She lives all alone in this little house. Well, almost alone—she has three cats. She can't walk very well because her legs are kind of stiff. Everybody calls her Grandma."

Mary Jane knocked at the door. "Come in!" a voice called. As they walked into the kitchen, they saw flashes of gray and white. "It's all right, kitties," the voice said, "these little girls won't hurt you."

Grandma Deller was sitting at the kitchen table. She looked as jolly as she was fat. A cane hung on the back of her chair.

Mary Jane introduced Dorothy to Grandma Deller. They gave Grandma the cake, and she asked them to thank Mary Jane's mother for it. The girls petted the cats. They talked and laughed with Grandma. Then they went back through the hedge to Mary Jane's house.

Later, snug in bed, Mary Jane and Dorothy were whispering to each other. "I like Grandma Deller," Dorothy said.

"I knew you would," said Mary Jane.

"And I'd like to see her cats again," Dorothy added.

"Maybe we can visit her tomorrow," said Mary Jane. "Mother says she gets lonesome. Most of the time she has to stay in her house. Sometimes Mother buys her groceries for her."

"Maybe we can go to the store for her tomorrow," Dorothy said, "or help her in the house."

"That would be fun," agreed Mary Jane.

The two girls whispered on about their plans for the next day until at last they fell asleep.

Do You Know?

Jesus once told his disciples a story. He said there will come a time when people will be judged for the kind of lives they have lived. There will be many who will be surprised on that day to hear the King say to them, "When I was hungry, you fed me. When I was thirsty, you gave me something to drink. When I was lonely and a stranger, you made me feel welcome. I had no clothes and you gave some to me. I was sick and you came to visit me."

These people will ask the King, "When did we see you hungry and feed you? When were you thirsty and we gave you a drink? When were you a stranger to us and we made you welcome? When did you have no clothes and we gave you some? When were you sick and we visited you?"

The King will answer, "When you were helping other people, you were also helping me."

Do you know that many people in the world are hungry today? In America we have food we can share with others, but it takes money to send it to them. Through our church we can give gifts to help feed hungry people in other parts of the world.

Do you know that enough powdered milk can be bought for a

few cents to feed many thirsty children in other countries?

Do you know someone who has just moved to your town and who needs to find a friend? Have you invited him to your church?

Do you know if you have some good outgrown clothes like shirts, socks, dresses, blue jeans, or shoes you can share with others? There are boys and girls being cared for in children's homes and missions of our church who need good used clothing. They also need school supplies, toys, books, and games.

Do you know someone who is sick or old? Can you visit him at his home? A little gift you make or buy to take to him or to send to him if he is in a hospital will make him happy.

Do you know that when you help others in these and other ways, you are obeying the teachings of Jesus?

PRAYER
Dear God, please help me to find ways I can help others. Amen.

First Week | Saturday

SCRIPTURE READING
Find and read Matthew 25:31–40 in the Bible. What are some ways you can help hungry, thirsty, lonely or sick people?

SECOND WEEK

Helping Others

Helping at Home

Gary opened one eye and looked at the clock on the bureau. Yes, that was the time he got up on school days, but this was Sunday. He wished he could sleep an extra hour on Sunday the way Mom and Dad did. What a long wait for breakfast! Yesterday Mom had breakfast almost ready at this time.

Suddenly Gary sat up in bed, exclaiming, "Why can't I—" Then he clapped his hand over his mouth. He mustn't wake up anyone and spoil his idea.

Quietly Gary slid out of bed and put on his socks. Even his slippers might make a little noise. He peered around the door. No one was in the hall. It was safe to go to the kitchen.

Here Gary stopped to think. What came first? Plates and cups and saucers, he decided, taking them out of the cupboard. Now the glasses for milk and juice from the other cupboard. And silver from the drawer. Oops! he nearly dropped it all! That would have waked up the whole house. Anything forgotten? Yes, the paper napkins. He folded them neatly to stand up on the plates.

Just then Gary heard the newspaper boy outside. Remembering the squeak in the door, he opened it carefully and picked up

the paper. As he did, he noticed the pansies growing by the steps. Wouldn't Mom like some flowers on the table? Of course! So he put the pansies in the center of the table and laid the newspaper at Dad's place.

With giant steps Gary tiptoed back to his room. He slipped into bed again. As he thought about his secret, he wriggled happily. No one would ever, ever guess that he had gone to the kitchen and all alone set the table for breakfast. But maybe he would tell Mom—sometime.

Second Week | Monday

A HYMN TO READ OR SING
Now thank we all our God
With heart and hands and voices,
Who wondrous things hath done,
In whom his world rejoices,
Who, from our mothers' arms,
Hath blessed us on our way
With countless gifts of love,
And still is ours today.

—*Martin Rinckart*

Second Week | Tuesday

HELPING AT CHURCH

Andy stood by the desk of the church secretary, Mrs. Davis. "Mother asked me to bring this to you, Mrs. Davis," he said. "It is the list of the women who will take part in the Lenten service next week."

"Thank you very much, Andy," said Mrs. Davis. "I was waiting to hear from your mother. I must finish those Lenten programs as soon as I can."

Andy turned to go, but Mrs. Davis called, "Wait, Andy! Were you at junior choir practice?"

"Yes," said Andy.

"Did Mr. Jim say at which Wednesday night service your choir will be singing?"

"Uh–huh," Andy nodded, "but I forget which."

"I might have known it," laughed Mrs. Davis. "I'll call Mr. Jim myself and find out."

Mrs. Davis picked up the telephone receiver and then put it down again. "There is one other thing, Andy," she said. "Do you have any extra time this afternoon? I'm in a big hurry to make out that Lenten program. But this morning I noticed that a great

many of the pencils in the pew racks of the church have broken points. Some of the racks need more visitor's cards too. Would you be able to help me for a while, sharpening pencils and putting cards in the racks?"

Andy hestitated. Mother had said to come right home. But Mrs. Davis needed him here at the church. "OK, Mrs. Davis," Andy decided, "I'll call Mother and ask her if I can help you."

Andy's mother was glad for him to help Mrs. Davis. He went right to work collecting the broken pencils. He found plenty. In fact, he had to empty the shavings out of the sharpener three times. He lost only one pencil. While he was talking to Mrs. Davis about rocket ships, one nice long pencil disappeared into space except for the very last inch!

Andy put the other pencils back where he had found them. Then he put more visitor's cards in the racks. "What else can I do?" he asked Mrs. Davis. "I like to work in the church."

"Do you really like to help?" she asked. "That's all for today, but sometimes I need a boy to run errands. And Mr. Jenner, who keeps our church clean, said he wished someone would help him wash the chalk boards and scrub the paste and crayola marks off the church school tables. There are lots of jobs to do."

"OK," said Andy, "I'll let you know when I can come and help you again, and you can tell me what needs to be done."

PRAYER

O God, thank you for all the people who help with the work of our church. I want to find ways to help too. Amen.

Second Week | Wednesday

HELPING OUR NEIGHBORS

Mrs. Shaw was sitting on her front porch. She rocked as she chatted with her visitor. "I hope you will be happy in our town, Mrs. Allen. I am quite sure you will like this neighborhood. There really is a friendly spirit here. Even the youngsters have it."

Mrs. Shaw waved to the boy coming out of the house next door. "Look at David there! Once a month he and his friends collect all the old newspapers in the neighborhood. The boys sell the newspapers to a used rug and paper dealer, and their Cub Scout pack sends the money to the United Nations Children's Fund. The boys help their neighbors and those children too."

"They can have ours too. Old papers clutter up the basement in no time. Please ask them to stop at our house next month," said Mrs. Allen.

Mrs. Shaw continued to rock back and forth. "When your grandchildren come to visit, Mrs. Allen," she said, "you will be glad that Shirley Jameson lives near you. She is only eight years old, but she is a little mother to the small children in that part of our neighborhood. She is responsible and can be counted on to take good care of them. I can tell you the mothers are grateful to have a neighbor like that."

"I'll remember Shirley when my grandchildren come," said Mrs. Allen with a chuckle. "They're still pretty little and they are so lively that someone has to keep an eye on them all the time. I can't wait to meet Shirley and David."

(to be continued)

Second Week | Thursday

HELPING OUR NEIGHBORS (continued)

"After hearing about David and Shirley," said Mrs. Allen, "I can't help wondering if all the children around here are little angels."

Mrs. Shaw laughed. "Now don't get me wrong! Of course these children all have their faults, but they can think up neighborly things to do. Take my grandson Alvin. He lives next door to Mr. and Mrs. Prester. Mr. Prester is seventy-two years old, and he has to be careful because his heart is not very strong. In the winter Alvin shovels the snow off Mr. Prester's sidewalk. He won't let Mr. Prester pay him for it because he knows the old man doesn't have much money, but that boy never refuses any of Mrs. Prester's cookies or cake! He's hollow!"

"I'm glad to hear there's a boy around who might shovel our walks," said Mrs. Allen. "Will you please ask Alvin if he can use a paying customer?"

Mrs. Shaw leaned forward in her chair to watch a boy on a bicycle turn the corner. "That's Ted Morgan," she said. "A few years ago a family from Germany moved into the little house on

that corner. By this summer they had saved enough money to take a vacation trip to their old home in Germany. Ted kept their lawn mowed while they were away so that when they came back, their American home would look good to them."

Mrs. Shaw stopped rocking and stood up. "Now, Mrs. Allen," she asked, "how about a cup of coffee?"

"Yes, thank you," replied Mrs. Allen, "and thank you for introducing me to my new neighbors!"

PRAYER

O God, may our eyes be open and our minds alert to find things we can do for others. Amen.

BLESS THOU THE GIFTS
Bless Thou the gifts our hands have brought!
Bless Thou the work our hearts have planned;
Ours is the faith, the will, the thought;
The rest, O God, is in Thy hand. Amen.

—Samuel Longfellow

So long as people anywhere are in need, we Christians feel we must do all we can to help them. But many times when we have done all we know it is not enough. So we ask God to bless our efforts.

The word *bless* has several meanings. The writer of this song uses the word to ask God to work through our gifts with his great love and power so they can accomplish what we hoped. We trust God to do this.

When you sing this offering prayer think what these words mean.

Second Week | *Saturday*

SCRIPTURE READING

Read Galatians 6: 10 from the Bible. "The household of faith" means the church. We could say this verse in another way—whenever we can, we should do good to everyone, and try especially to help one another.

22

THIRD WEEK

Worshiping Together

Third Week | Sunday

WHY CHRISTIANS WORSHIP TOGETHER IN THE CHURCH

The most important thing we do together in the church is to worship God. We love and worship him because he first loved us, and sent his Son Jesus Christ to help us understand this. And we love him because in our hearts and minds we need to love him. He has made us this way.

Each man and woman, each boy and girl can worship God by himself. Each of us should have a quiet time to pray, to read the Bible, to read a book like this, and to think about God. But as Christians we believe that we must also come together each Sunday to worship God in our own church.

You have read the stories of a number of people who came to know God and believe in him. Some lived long ago in Bible times. Some are living today. These people are all a part of the Christian church.

It is the church—God's people—who have told the story of his love and faithfulness through all the years. It is the church that has brought the story of Jesus to you and to me.

When people worship together in church they are helped to live as people of God.

Third Week | Monday

We Turn Our Thoughts to God

Sometimes when we come to church our minds are full of many things—coasting, a game, a good dinner, or school—so at the beginning of the service of worship we are reminded why we have come together. The organ prelude helps us to be quiet and to turn our thoughts to God. We sing a hymn of praise. The minister offers a brief prayer, or repeats a verse of scripture.

Often he uses words from the psalms such as these:

> I was glad when they said to me,
>> "Let us go to the house of the Lord!"
>>> *—Psalm 122:1*
>
> I lift up my eyes to the hills.
>> From whence does my help come?
> My help comes from the Lord,
>> who made heaven and earth.
>>> *—Psalm 121:1–2*

Then we are ready to pray together a brief prayer in which we ask God to forgive us for any wrongdoing and to prepare our minds and hearts so that we may worship him rightly.

We Praise and Thank God

In the church service we bring our praise and thanks to God. Praising God is telling how great and wonderful he is. It is remembering all he does for us, and thanking him for it. Often we do this by singing a hymn of praise like "Holy, Holy, Holy."

Sometimes the minister reads words like these from Psalm 105:

> O give thanks to the LORD, call on his name,
>> make known his deeds among the peoples!
> Sing to him, sing praises to him,
>> tell of all his wonderful works!

Verses which thank God are found in Psalm 136:

> O give thanks to the LORD, for he is good,
>> for his steadfast love endures for ever.
> O give thanks to the God of gods,
>> for his steadfast love endures for ever.

Find Psalm 136 in the Bible and read verses 3–9.

WE PRAY TO GOD

Prayer is the most important part of worship. Prayer is thinking about God and feeling close to him. It is listening to him or speaking with him about our most important thoughts and ideas. God speaks to us through our own minds, and in many different ways.

In the prayer which the minister prays in the church service he tries to include what all the people need and what they would like to have him pray for. At the same time each person prays silently, in his own heart. Each one thinks about what the minister is saying. Each one also prays his own prayers.

Jesus spent much time in prayer. Do you remember that when the disciples saw how much Jesus depended on prayer to help him, they asked him to teach them to pray?

In reply to their request, Jesus taught them the prayer we now call "The Lord's Prayer." You can find this yourself in the Bible. It is in the book of Matthew. Find Chapter 6, and read verses 9 through 13.

We pray this prayer together in the church service. It is a prayer that each one of us can pray every day.

Third Week | *Thursday*

We Learn What God Wants of Us

There are many stories in our Bible that help us understand the Christian way to do things. Some are stories about Jesus who "went about doing good." Others are stories Jesus told. We have already read a few of the stories. Here are two other short stories from the Bible for you to read.

The Good Samaritan   Luke 10:30–37
The Widow's Mite   Mark 12:41–44

To find these stories first look in the index to see where Luke or Mark begins. Turn to that page and then keep going until you find the chapter you are looking for. Run your finger down the column until you find the right verse. Read from that verse through the last verse of the reference.

In our service of worship the verses read from the Bible and the sermon teach us how to be better Christians. In the sermon the minister explains what the Bible verses mean. He tries to help us discover the things God wants us to do.

Sometimes the minister tells stories as part of his longer sermon. The next time you are in church listen for these stories. Perhaps you will want to talk about them with your parents after church.

PRAYER

O God, thank you for the stories about Jesus that we can read in the Bible. Help us to understand them and to know what we should do. Amen.

Third Week | Friday

WE GO OUT TO SERVE GOD

We can think about God at any time, but it helps us all to be in the church service worshiping him together. At the close of the service the minister in his prayer and benediction prays that God will be with us wherever we go and whatever we do. He sometimes uses these words:

The LORD bless you and keep you:
The LORD make his face to shine upon you, and be gracious to
  you:
The LORD lift up his countenance upon you, and give you
  peace.

—Numbers 6:24–26

The word "countenance" means face.

Perhaps you will want to use some of these verses when you worship alone.

PRAYER

Dear God, be with us in all that we do and wherever we may go. Help us to remember you always. Amen.

A HYMN TO READ OR SING
O Praise Ye the Lord

Paraphrase of Psalm 150   *Theme from César Franck*

Vigorously

1 O praise ye the Lord, Praise him in his tem - ple!
2 O praise ye the Lord, Praise him on the trum - pet!
3 With cym - bals and drum And tim - brels and or - gan,

O praise ye the Lord, Praise him for his migh - ty acts!
O praise ye the Lord, Praise him with the dance and song!
Let all things that breathe In mu - sic O praise the Lord!

Stanzas 2 and 3 arranged by Junior Vacation School, Richmond Hill Methodist Church, New York, July, 1944.
From *The Whole World Singing*, compiled by Edith Lovell Thomas. Copyright, 1950, by
Friendship Press, Inc.

FOURTH WEEK

Living as Christians

A Christian Is Forgiving

"Wow! It's snowing!"

Tommy jumped out of bed and pressed his nose against the window to see better. The first big snow of the season was falling. Tommy knew what he was going to do today. He was going to try out his Christmas sled.

After breakfast he put on his boots and bundled himself up in his warm coat, the cap that came down over his ears, and his red mittens. He pulled the new sled to the top of the hill. Other boys were already there—bigger boys whom Tommy did not know.

"Hey, look!" one of the boys shouted when he saw Tommy. "He's got a new sled. Can I try it, kid? Oh, come on, just once!"

Another boy grabbed the sled and yanked it away from Tommy. "We won't hurt it," he called back as he flung himself on it and whizzed down the hill.

Tommy jumped up and down and yelled, "Give me my sled! I haven't had a ride on it yet!"

The older boys just laughed. They were too big for Tommy. They made him keep out of the way while they had fun with his

sled. Now he could not use it at all! Angrily he watched the other boys.

"I guess you'd like to have your sled, wouldn't you?" the biggest boy teased.

Tommy nodded, but he knew the boys weren't ready yet to let him coast. "Is it fun?" he asked.

"Keen," said the other boy.

But somehow using Tommy's sled didn't seem such fun to the big boys any more. "Here, kid," they said, "you can have it now." Tommy looked the sled over carefully. He saw that the runners weren't bent or the wood scratched. The boys started to walk away.

"Hey!" Tommy called after them. He had been afraid of the boys, but now that they were going away, the hill looked awfully steep to him. "Maybe we could take turns."

The boys came back. "We're sorry now that we took your sled. Aren't you mad at us?"

"Would you coast down the hill with me?" asked Tommy.

"Do you really want us to? No hard feelings?"

"No hard feelings," said Tommy.

So Tommy sat up front on the sled. One of the older boys sat behind him with his legs around Tommy and steered the sled. They all had fun for the rest of the morning.

PRAYER

Dear God, it is hard for us not to be mad or hurt when someone does something we do not like. Help us to remember that it is better to make friends and to share with them than to keep what we have to ourselves. Help us to be forgiving. Amen.

Fourth Week | Monday

SCRIPTURE READING

Read 1 Corinthians 13:4–7. To find this passage look in the index for the page where 1 Corinthians begins. Turn to that page and keep going until you find chapter 13. Read verses 4, 5, 6, and 7. Then read the middle part of verse 5 once more. Think about what this means.

A Christian Does Not Insist on His Own Way

Don and Dan are eight-year-old twins, but they don't look alike and they don't think alike. They usually do different things too. Don wants to play with the other boys. Dan would rather work with his chemistry set or read a library book. There is just one way the twins are exactly alike—they both like to watch television.

The same programs? No! After school Dan wants to watch a program about rockets and space travel called "Away to the

Moon." Don likes to see cowboys in "Frontier Days." The two programs are on at the same time. That makes a problem!

Dan thinks the family ought to have another TV set. Then he and Don could each watch his own favorite program. But their father says it would cost too much to buy another TV set.

On some days there is no trouble. When Don goes to his friend Tom's house after school, he watches "Frontier Days" there. Dan has the TV set at home all to himself for "Away to the Moon."

On other days there *is* trouble. If it is rainy or cold, both boys come straight home from school. The first one in the house tunes in the channel for his program. Then his brother arrives pell-mell and insists on changing to the other channel. Back and forth they switch from one channel to the other. Before long they are both angry, each one trying to shove the other out of the way. Neither Don nor Dan sees enough of his program to know what is going on.

Have you ever wanted to do something at the same time when somebody else wanted to do something different? What happened? How do you think the boys might solve their problem?

PRAYER

Our Father, help us to be fair with others and to take turns. Help us not to insist on having our own way. Amen.

Fourth Week | Wednesday

A CHRISTIAN IS TRUTHFUL

"My cake—my beautiful cake!"

Joel could hear his mother's voice clearly. He was in the basement, playing with his train.

"Who touched my cake? Somebody's been testing the frosting. I'd just like to know who poked those holes in it!" Her voice sounded very cross. Joel's mother had worked hard to make her cake beautiful for the women's meeting.

Judy, Joel's five-year-old sister, came into the kitchen. Her face and hands were streaked with chocolate frosting just like the frosting on the cake.

"Oh, Judy!" exclaimed her mother. "Did you spoil my cake?"

Judy shook her head, "No."

"Those look like your finger marks on the cake, and you have frosting all over yourself. How can you say you didn't do it?"

"But, Mummy, I didn't," Judy insisted.

"Judy, it's bad enough that my cake is spoiled, but if you say you didn't do it when I can see you did, I'll have to spank you."

Judy began to cry.

When Joel went up to the kitchen from the basement, he saw

the tears rolling down his sister's cheeks. He knew the finger marks on the cake were his. Judy was telling the truth. She had only licked the pan their mother had made the frosting in.

If you were Joel, would you say anything?

Prayer

Our Father, sometimes it is hard for us to be truthful. Please help us not to be afraid to tell the truth. Amen.

Fourth Week | *Thursday*

A CHRISTIAN IS THANKFUL

Read Psalm 75:1. Think of things for which you wish to thank God and write your own prayer of thanksgiving.

Fourth Week | *Friday*

A CHRISTIAN IS PATIENT

"Mother, aren't people who go to church supposed to be good?" Sherry asked.

"Now that *is* a question!" said her mother. "I think most church people try to do what they think is right, but there are times when we all make mistakes. No one is as good as he should be. What makes you ask such a thing anyway?"

"Well, there's a boy in our church school class—"

"Oh," nodded her mother, "I know that you girls think boys are a bother."

"But Mother," said Sherry, "it's not just that. The boys tease us and we girls get mad at them, but we don't mind it too much. This new boy does things none of the other boys would do."

"What kind of things?" her mother asked.

"Well, Mr. Gardner gave us some questions last Sunday and I

42

saw this boy copy all of the answers from another boy's paper. He never listens when anyone else is talking. Today Mr. Jackson visited our class and the new boy was rude to him. Mr. Gardner has to sit next to him during worship to keep him quiet. He is just a bad boy!"

"It sounds as if he has many things to learn yet," said her mother. "What else do you know about him? What are his father and mother like? Does he have any brothers or sisters? Did he just move to our town?"

Sherry looked at her mother in surprise. "I don't know," she said. "Why would I want to find out those things?"

"It might help you understand why he acts the way he does," her mother replied. "Perhaps he isn't happy at home. Or perhaps he is just lonely and needs friends."

"He doesn't want to be friends," objected Sherry.

"Well, of course you can't make this boy like you," her mother said, "but has your class really tried to be friends with him?"

"Sometimes we have teased him," Sherry admitted. "I guess we could be more friendly."

"It is worth trying," said her mother. "Perhaps your friendliness will encourage him to be more friendly. But he won't change all of a sudden. You will need to be patient with him. In the church we try to understand and to help one another. We try to be patient with those who haven't yet learned to live as Jesus taught."

Fourth Week / Saturday

A CHRISTIAN IS JOYFUL

A HYMN TO READ OR SING
All people that on earth do dwell,
Sing to the Lord with cheerful voice;
Him serve with mirth, his praise forth tell,
Come ye before him and rejoice.
—*William Kethe*

FIFTH WEEK

Christian Adventures of Long Ago

Fifth Week | Sunday

SOME ADVENTURE STORIES

Many Christians have been people of great courage. They have done things and gone places no one else dared. They have risked their lives to tell people of God's love. Some were beaten, others thrown into prison, and still others burned at the stake. But the strange thing is that the more dangerous it was to live as Jesus taught, the stronger the church became. God has always given his people strength to do his work and the church has grown.

God brought the church into being through the life, death, and resurrection of Jesus Christ who is the Lord of the church. Jesus' disciples were leaders when the church began, and since their time many other people have been leaders in the church. In the next few pages you will find stories of some of the people who have helped the church grow. From a small group of believers, the church has grown until it includes people around the world.

Fifth Week | Monday

ADVENTURES OF A LETTER-WRITER

If you will look at the books in the New Testament, beginning

with Romans, you will discover that many of them are letters written by Paul.

Paul was one of the first Christians. He was not one of Jesus' disciples, but he knew some of the disciples. Do you remember what you have learned about him? At first he was against the Christians, but when he found out more about them and about Jesus, he too wanted to be a Christian.

Paul was the first missionary. He felt his one big job was to tell everyone that Jesus was God's gift of love to all people. Paul traveled a great deal, sometimes to places far from his home. He went from town to town preaching to the people and helping them to start their own churches.

Because Paul could not visit these churches very often, he wrote letters to tell them more about Jesus, and to help them with their problems. Even though these letters were written long ago, they help us, too, to understand what Jesus taught.

Paul had many adventures and narrow escapes. He mentions some of these in his second letter to the church in Corinth:

"Five times I have received . . . the forty lashes less one. Three times I have been beaten with rods; once I was stoned. Three times I have been shipwrecked; a night and a day I have been adrift at sea; on frequent journeys, in . . . danger from robbers, danger from my own people, . . . danger in the city, danger in the wilderness, danger at sea, . . . in toil and hardship, through many a sleepless night, in hunger and thirst, often without food, in cold and exposure." (2 Corinthians 11:24–27)

Wherever Paul went he preached about Jesus, even when his enemies ordered him not to. He started churches and told the story of Jesus to many, many people.

PRAYER

Dear God, our Father, thank you for people like Paul who were strong and brave and helped the church to grow. Give us courage like theirs so we can take our part in the church. Amen.

Fifth Week | *Tuesday*

AN ADVENTURE OF MARTIN LUTHER

Many years after Paul lived, but still a long time ago, there lived a brave Christian named Martin Luther.

By Luther's time the Christian church had become bigger. Now there were many churches in many different countries.

But some of the leaders in the church were living and teaching in a way different from that the Bible taught. Martin Luther believed some things they were doing were wrong.

Luther wrote down in a long list the things he thought should be changed. He nailed this list on the church door where everyone could read it. He preached about these things. There were many people who agreed with him. They were glad that Martin Luther was speaking and writing in this way.

But the church leaders were very angry. They threatened that they would put him out of the church unless he appeared before

them within sixty days and explained the things he was teaching. His friends said, "Don't go. It may be a trap. If you go to the meeting your enemies may arrest you and even put you to death."

But Luther said, "I believe that what I have been teaching is the truth as I read it in the Bible. I will go to the meeting."

He did go. The church leaders had before them a pile of books Luther had written. They asked him questions, and he told them what he believed. The church leaders did not agree with him. They said, "You must say that you are wrong. You must take back what you have written in your books. If you do, we will not put you out of the church."

"Unless you can prove I am wrong by the Bible," Martin Luther replied, "I will not take back my words." When they could not do so, he said, "Here I stand. I cannot do otherwise. May God help me!" This made the church leaders very angry at him.

Martin Luther escaped from his enemies. Because Luther and his friends had been put out of the church, they started one of their own. It came to be called the Lutheran Church and was one of the first of the Protestant churches. The word "Protestant" means that we speak up for the things we believe about Jesus and the Bible.

O God, help us to do the things we should in our church. Help us to know what pleases you and what does not. Help us to understand how others worship you, and help us all to love you. Amen.

Fifth Week / Wednesday

AN ADVENTURE ON THE MAYFLOWER

"Land ho!" shouted the lookout on the Mayflower.

The Pilgrims crowded on deck. Some had thought they would never see land again. For two months the ship had been storm-tossed on a wide and empty ocean. They strained their eyes. It *was* land—flat, and covered with woods.

The captain looked at his map. "Tonight we will anchor offshore," he said. "Tomorrow I will find you a safe harbor on the other side."

The next morning the captain set sail around the tip of Cape Cod. The excited passengers talked of nothing but the new land. "Where shall we settle?" they wondered. "What shall we do first?"

Most of the Pilgrims had come across the ocean to be free to worship God with the Bible as their guide. But a few men who

had joined the ship just before it sailed wanted only to get rich. "Once we are off this ship," they nów bragged, "we shall go where we please and do as we like."

Elder William Brewster was disturbed by their boasts. He asked Edward Winslow, "How can we survive if we do not all stay together and work together?"

Winslow replied, "It is a matter that we must talk over with some of the others."

These men met in the cabin of the ship. Elder Brewster told what he had overheard. "Our undertaking will fail," he insisted, "unless we pledge ourselves to think of the good of all."

"We should make an agreement to live together under laws that everyone will obey," said Carver.

The other men decided that this was the right thing to do. They wrote out an agreement while the captain was bringing the ship into the safe waters of Cape Cod Bay. When the Mayflower dropped her anchor, they joined the other Pilgrims on deck. Everybody knelt and thanked God for delivering them from the dangers of the ocean.

Then Elder Brewster asked every man on board to come to the ship's cabin. He explained to them the need for the agreement.

William Bradford put the paper on the table. One by one the men signed it.

This agreement was the Mayflower Compact. It was signed on November 11, 1620. It helped the Pilgrims to survive after they settled at Plymouth.

Did you know that these Pilgrims became members of the first Congregational church in America? This was the beginning of one of the parts of our United Church of Christ.

PRAYER

God our Father, we thank you for the brave Christians who have come before us. Help us to be unafraid if we are needed to do things that are new and strange. Help us to work together in our church as Jesus would have us do. Amen.

The Liberty Bell's Adventure

The bells in Philadelphia were ringing out good news on July 4, 1776. People were shouting the news in the streets too. No more British rule! Our country was a new nation—the United States of America! The Declaration of Independence said so.

The bell that rang the loudest was the big one in the state house. On it were words from the Bible: "Proclaim liberty throughout all the land unto all the inhabitants thereof." (Leviticus 25:10b, King James Version) The big bell did that on the fourth of July in 1776. So people began to call it the Liberty Bell.

Did you know this famous bell was once almost captured? You can see it in Philadelphia now only because brave men saved it from the British in the war that followed the Declaration of Independence.

The British army won many battles in the first year of the war. Between victories the enemy soldiers collected all the metal they could find and melted it down to make more cannon balls. Closer and closer they marched to Philadelphia. If only they could get their hands on the big Liberty Bell! Its two thousand pounds of metal would make many cannon balls.

"We must hide the Liberty Bell," men in Philadelphia said, "where the British will never find it."

"But where?" someone asked. "It is so big and heavy. How can we hide it?"

A man spoke up, "I know the pastor of the Zion Reformed Church in the village of Allentown. Pastor Blumer might let us hide the bell in his church."

"If he will," said another man, "we can ask John Mickley to take the bell there in his farm wagon."

Farmers often came to Philadelphia with wagon loads of vegetables and other things to sell. One day when John Mickley was ready to go back home, he drove his empty wagon slowly to the state house. At a signal he turned aside and stopped. Men quickly loaded the Liberty Bell on his wagon and covered it with sacks of potatoes. In minutes John was on his way again. He joined the other farm wagons leaving Philadelphia. Any enemy on the road would see just a wagon load of potatoes.

The horses pulled the heavy load easily. Then the wagon suddenly broke down. The men with John tried hard, but they could not fix the wagon. They knew the enemy soldiers were marching nearer. "Quick!" urged Frederick Leaser, another farmer. "Put the bell on my wagon! I'll take it the rest of the way."

At the Allentown church the pastor took them inside and pointed out where to pry up the floor boards. The men hurried to lower the big bell into the space beneath the floor. Then they put the boards back into place.

The bell stayed hidden there in the church until it could safely ring again in Philadelphia. The British made no cannon balls from our Liberty Bell!

Note: If you are ever in Allentown, you will want to visit the Liberty Bell Shrine in Zion United Church of Christ. This shrine was built in 1962, on the very spot where the bell was hidden, to help everyone remember the Liberty Bell's adventure.

Fifth Week | Friday

PRAYER

Dear God, we are glad for our country and for our churches where we are free to worship as we think right. Help us to be good citizens of our country and good members of our church. Amen.

An Adventure in a Haystack

"Sam, are you on your way to the grove?" asked Samuel Mills' friends.

It was the summer of 1806. Some of the boys at Williams College met every Saturday in a grove of maple trees to talk and pray together. On this hot afternoon only four of Sam's friends showed up.

"Look at those black clouds!" exclaimed one. "We're in for a storm."

Sam said, "If it rains, we can get under that haystack over there in the field."

The storm came on quickly with lightning and thunder. The boys ran for the haystack. Cows had nibbled at the hay and eaten out a kind of cave at the bottom of the stack. All five boys could sit there, safe and dry in the pouring rain.

They began to talk about faraway places. Traders who went to Asia had brought back many stories about the people there.

"Just think of it," Harvey said, "the people in Asia have never heard of God or of the Bible!"

"You know what I'd like to do?" Sam asked. "I'd like to go

there and tell the people about God."

James nodded his head. "Yes, I seem to keep hearing Jesus say, 'Go into all the world and preach the gospel.'"

"But can we do it?" they asked. "We are just college boys. We don't have much money for traveling. We wouldn't know how to go about it."

"We *can* do it if we *will*," said Sam.

"God needs us to do his work," James insisted. "If we really want to do it, God will help us to do it."

Other church members were also concerned about the people who did not know of God. They gave the needed money. The five young men who talked and prayed under that haystack were the first missionaries sent from America to other countries.

PRAYER

Dear God, help us to remember that there are many things we can do for you if we really want to. Please help us to want to do them. Amen.

SIXTH WEEK

Thinking About the Church

WHAT IS A CHURCH?

"The church is a place to sleep," said Bobby Bat as he hung upside down in his corner of the steeple.

"I think the church is where you eat," said Chuckie Churchmouse, "especially after the ladies have been working in the kitchen. Then there are good crumbs here and there. Yummy!"

"To me the church is a place to make pretty," said Flora Flower. "It is colorful and makes me think thoughts of beauty."

Sonny Sunshine agreed. "I think the church is a bright warm spot. It is very comfortable."

"Hold on, Sonny," stepped in Buddy Book. "I live in the library back here in your church. There are some things between my pages that are not meant to make one comfortable. I make people think. Sometimes they think about things they should not have done, and then they are not comfortable."

"Righto, Buddy! When people sit on me each Sunday I don't want them to fall asleep like Bobby Bat," added Benny Bench.

"Let's not worry about that. I think the church is something very quiet," said Clara Clock. "Often I make all the noise there is."

"Don't forget, though, when I go through the organ pipes I can make the most beautiful music ever," said Windy Breeze.

"I make music too," added Billy Bell. "I call people to worship God in the church. That's what a church is—a place to worship."

"You have said many things about the church," said Christine Christian. "Each of you has said the church is something like yourselves. I am a person. I believe the church is people—people who love God. There were people long ago who loved God and tried to live as Jesus taught, and these people were part of the church. The Bible tells about some of them. People in the church today try to do what God wants. Yes, that's the answer I would give. The church is people—people who love God."

Sixth Week / Monday

WHAT IS MY CHURCH CALLED?

Do you know the name of your church? Is it St. John? Trinity? Pilgrim? First Church? Or what? Is there more to its name? Do you know what the United Church of Christ is?

When the disciples started teaching and preaching in the homes of the people, it was not long before church members became known as "Christians." At first this name was used to make fun of them. But now we are very proud to be called Christians—people who are followers of Jesus Christ.

After Martin Luther's adventure the church divided into many groups. Some of these groups came to our country.

The Pilgrims and the Puritans were the first Congregational group in America. A little later in New England other people began the Christian Church. People from Germany and Switzerland came to Pennsylvania bringing with them their Reformed Church. Other German people came to this country and settled in Missouri. They worshiped in Evangelical Churches. They sent missionary pastors like Joseph Rieger up and down the river to preach to the new settlers.

In 1957 these four churches joined together in one new church, called the United Church of Christ. We belong to this church. We have united because we want to be Christians together.

Sixth Week / Tuesday

MY CHURCH WORKS WITH OTHERS

There are other churches that were started at about the same time as the four mentioned above. The Methodist, the Presbyterian, the Baptist, the Lutheran, and many others began after Martin Luther so bravely stood up for what he believed was right. These are Protestant churches.

Usually the Protestant churches in a town do some things together. They may join in services on Thanksgiving or Good Friday. Sometimes they hold a vacation church school for all the boys and girls who wish to attend.

Protestants together help other people through Church World Service. You may have given clothing or money for this.

Even though these churches are different in some ways, in all of them people love God, and try to obey the teachings of Jesus.

Sixth Week / Wednesday

SCRIPTURE READING

In Matthew 28: 19–20, you can read something Jesus told his disciples to do. We believe he speaks to us today too, asking us to teach all people about God's great love.

Sixth Week / Thursday

WAYS THE CHURCH WORKS

Churches work in many ways to carry out the commandment

of Jesus you read in Matthew 28. You may know about some of these ways already. Here are some of the things our church does:

Our church tells others about God, both in our own country and in other lands. There are people who cannot read the stories from the Bible for themselves. Our church builds schools to help people like this and sends teachers to help them learn to read and write.

Our church shows farmers how to grow better crops, and how to dig wells so they can have water for their homes and their gardens.

Our church helps people get well. The church has built many hospitals. These help people know that the church cares about them when they are ill.

Our church cares for boys and girls whose parents cannot take care of them.

It cares for people when they are older and cannot take care of themselves.

Our church has colleges and other schools where people can find out how God works in his world. Teachers, scientists, doctors, lawyers, and many others study in our church's schools. Ministers, missionaries, and other church workers study there too.

Our church helps new congregations build their churches. Many new churches are needed near big cities where new homes are being built. Your church may be one of these new ones.

Some missionaries of our church help fishermen. Others help people who live in big cities. Still others work in the country with farmers or Indians. Wherever people need help, the church tries to send workers.

In all of these ways our own church is sharing the good news with others just as Jesus said to do. Everybody in the church can help in this work. Even you. That's why we find out about the people who are in need, give what we can to assist them, and pray for them. Together we carry out the commandment of Jesus found in Matthew 28:19–20.

WHAT KIND OF PEOPLE BELONG TO THE CHURCH?

"Hello, Tim."

Tim looked up to see who was calling him. He was racing down the sidewalk in his wagon he had made himself. "Engine No. 9" was painted on the side. Tim was playing his favorite game of "fireman." He stopped just in time to keep from running into Mr. Jackson, the minister at his church.

"Hello, Mr. Jackson," said Tim when he caught his breath. "I was playing I was going to a fire."

"Are you going to be a fireman when you grow up?" asked the minister.

"Sure," said Tim. Then he frowned. "But I suppose you'd rather that I would be a preacher, or something Christian."

"Why Tim, what do you mean?" laughed Mr. Jackson. "Someday you may want to be a minister or another kind of church worker, but don't you think firemen can be Christian?"

"Can they?" asked Tim in surprise.

"Why sure," said Mr. Jackson. "Being a Christian doesn't mean that we have to sit in church all day. We can show love for God by being helpful wherever we are."

"Firemen help people by putting out fires," said Tim.

"That's right," said Mr. Jackson. "Who else helps people?"

"Well, the policeman helps me across the street. The doctor helps me get well when I'm sick. The garage man fixes Dad's car when something goes wrong."

"Now you're thinking," said Mr. Jackson. "And don't forget the farmers and the people who work in stores. Your dad works in a factory and makes things. Why don't you talk to some of the people at church next Sunday and find out what kind of jobs they have? You'll be surprised at how many different jobs there are."

"I'll do that, Mr. Jackson. Now I have to put out that fire. Good-bye," called Tim as he hurried off.

"Good-bye," called Mr. Jackson after him. "Do a good job!"

Sixth Week / Saturday

A Prayer for Our Church

Dear God:

We praise you for the many people who have been a part of the church—

For your son, Jesus, who taught people about you;

For the disciples who learned from him;

For the first Christians who dared to belong to the church even when they were in danger;

For all those who have told the story of Jesus and your love;

For the leaders of our own United Church of Christ who want to work together with Christians everywhere;

And for our own church where we worship and work with one another.

We thank you, God, that we also are a part of your great church.

Please guide and help us as we try to follow the teachings of Jesus, showing your love to others. Help us to understand what we are taught, and to do what we know is right.

We ask you to forgive us for times we have failed. Help us to be better Christians. Amen.

HOLY WEEK

Remembering Jesus

A Day of Praise

Jesus knew it was dangerous to go to Jerusalem. The leaders of the church were waiting to arrest him. They were angry at him for not keeping their rules. He healed people on the Sabbath, they said. He didn't love his own nation enough. He taught that God loved everyone, the Samaritans as well as the Jews.

Some of these leaders did mean and cruel things, and they realized that Jesus knew this. For this reason they were afraid of him.

But Jesus was not afraid. He believed it was right for him to take his message to Jerusalem. His mind was made up.

With great courage he rode into the city like a king in a triumphal procession, while many who knew and loved him shouted "Hosanna!" He chose to ride upon an ass—the beast kings rode when they came in peace. Some of his own people, and even one of his disciples, thought he should have chosen instead the horse of war. He took this way to tell his friends and his enemies once more that his message was one of peace and love.

You have known the story of Palm Sunday a long time. Now that you are older, perhaps you would like to read it as it is told in the Bible.

You will find it in Matthew 21:1–11.

Dear God, we thank you for the bravery of Jesus. Help us to do what we feel is right, even when it is hard. Amen.

Holy Week | Monday

IN THE TEMPLE

This was the week of the feast of the Passover, a Jewish holiday. The city was crowded, for all the Jewish people who could, came to the temple in Jerusalem to celebrate this feast. It reminded the people how Moses many years before had led their people out of Egypt where they had been slaves.

Jesus went to the temple to pray. Do you think he found it quiet and peaceful? Not at all. Jesus found the courtyard of the temple crowded with travelers. When they tried to buy animals for the temple sacrifices, the merchants charged them unfair prices. When they went to the money changers to exchange their own money for temple coins, they were cheated.

All this buying and selling and cheating made Jesus very angry. He drove out both those who were buying and those who were selling.

"Isn't this supposed to be a place where people can come to

worship God?" he asked. "You have made it a den of thieves."

You will find this story in Matthew 21:12–13.

Holy Week | *Tuesday*

A FRIEND BECOMES AN ENEMY

In the days that followed the excitement that Jesus had caused in the temple, he went about in Jerusalem talking to people and telling them about God's kingdom. Jesus often went back to the temple to pray and to talk with the crowds in the temple courtyard.

At the same time some of the religious leaders who were called chief priests were plotting against Jesus. They thought that his teachings were wrong. They wanted to get rid of him. They were afraid that the people would follow him instead of them.

They tried to catch him saying or doing something that was wrong. They watched him very closely. They asked him clever questions so that Jesus would be saying something wrong no matter how he answered them. But Jesus was even more clever in his replies, and they could not catch him that way.

Then Jesus' enemies had an idea. Perhaps one of Jesus' disciples would help them. Which one would it be? Peter? No, he was the leader of the disciples, next to Jesus. James or John? They too were loyal. So were all the others. Except, maybe, for one named Judas. He had been disappointed that Jesus had not wanted to be king.

One day Judas went to the chief priests and said that he was sure he could find some way to turn Jesus over to them. The chief priests said that they would pay Judas if he would do this. So it was agreed.

We don't know exactly why Judas did this, but the fact is that he did.

A friend had now become an enemy.

Prayer

O God, we do not always do the things we should. Sometimes we turn away from Jesus. Help us to want to do the things he would have us do. Amen.

Holy Week / *Wednesday*

PREPARING FOR THE PASSOVER

The Passover was to be celebrated on Friday. This festival always takes place in the home. Jesus and his disciples were visitors in Jerusalem, so the disciples asked him, "What are we going to do about the Passover? Where can we celebrate it?"

Jesus chose two of the disciples and said to them, "Go into the city. There you will meet a man carrying a jar of water. Follow him, and when he enters a house say to the owner of the house, 'Jesus wants to know where the guest room is where he is to celebrate the Passover with his disciples.'"

The two disciples did this, and the owner of the house showed them an upstairs room which they could use. In the evening Jesus came with the other disciples to share in a simple meal in preparation for the coming festival. Jesus alone knew it was to be their last supper together.

In those days people did not have shoes like ours. They either wore sandals or went barefoot. The roads and streets of Palestine were dusty, and before a person had walked very far his feet were quite dirty. When a person entered a house, usually a servant was waiting to wash his feet.

Jesus and his disciples did not have any servants. None of the disciples offered to wash the feet of the others. But Jesus himself got up from the meal, wrapped a towel around himself, poured water into a basin, and began to wash their feet.

When Jesus had finished, he sat down again and said to them, "Do you know what I have done to you? If I, who am your teacher, have washed your feet, then you ought to wash one another's feet." Jesus was showing them how they ought to serve one another.

PRAYER

O God, thank you for Jesus' example showing us how we ought to help one another. We would serve him and you by serving and loving one another. Amen.

Holy Week | Maundy Thursday

A DAY OF REMEMBRANCE

As Jesus and the disciples were eating together that Thursday evening, Jesus was wondering how he could help his friends to remember him. He knew by this time that one of the disciples was going to betray him. He knew that soon he was going to be put to death. In later years how would his followers remember him?

How could he help them to understand what was happening to him?

As they were eating, Jesus picked up one of the small, flat loaves of bread. Bread was a common thing that people ate at every meal.

Jesus said a prayer of thanks, and then he broke the bread into several pieces, and gave the pieces to his disciples. He said, "Take this bread and eat it. This is my body which is for you."

Then he took a cup of wine. This was also a common thing that people had at their meals in those days. Again Jesus prayed. Then he gave the cup to his disciples and they all drank some of the wine. Jesus said, "This is my blood, which will be poured out for many people for the forgiveness of sins." Then he said, "Do these things to help you remember me."

People in the church today still do as he asked that night. We now call this the Lord's supper, or holy communion. It recalls to us the things Jesus said and did. It makes his death upon the cross for all people real to us. It helps us know he is alive today.

Prayer

Dear God, we think about Jesus on this day. Help us to remember him always. Help us to be loving as he was, to serve as he served, and to live as he lived. Amen.

Holy Week | Good Friday

A Day of Sadness

After Jesus and his disciples finished supper on Thursday night, they went out into the darkness. Judas had already left.

Jesus and the disciples went to the Garden of Gethsemane, a quiet place where they often met to talk and plan. Jesus said to them, "Sit here, while I pray." They knew he was greatly troubled, but they still did not realize what was going to happen. They fell asleep while he was praying.

Jesus came and found them sleeping and said, "Could you not watch with me one hour?"

While he was speaking Judas came with a band of soldiers and men sent by the chief priests. Some carried torches and others swords and clubs.

Judas went up to Jesus at once and said, "Master!" Then he kissed him. This was the sign agreed upon to let Jesus' enemies know which one was Jesus.

They led Jesus to the high priest. When he said he was God's Son, they took him to the governor, a man named Pilate. It was now Friday morning. Pilate could not find that Jesus had done anything wrong, but a crowd of people were crying, "Crucify him!" Pilate was more eager to have the people like him than he was to help Jesus. He had Jesus scourged and handed him over to the soldiers to be crucified.

They took Jesus, and he went out, bearing his own cross, to a hill called Golgotha. There he was crucified. Even as he was suffering on the cross, he said, "Father, forgive them; for they know not what they do!"

Finally, after three hours, Jesus died. Jesus' friends were stunned and frightened. They were very sad. They did not know where to turn.

On Good Friday many churches hold a service of worship which lasts from noon until three o'clock, the hours Jesus was on the cross. Good Friday is a very solemn day.

Holy Week / *Saturday*

PRAYER

O God, we do not understand how people could crucify Jesus for being true to what he knew was right. And yet we know that sometimes we are cruel to each other.

We know that Jesus did not hesitate to face death so that we might understand your love. We give thanks to you that he triumphed over death, and that his presence is with us always.

We pray that you will forgive us if we have been cruel to one another. Help us to remember that you want us to love one another. Amen.

Holy Week / Easter Sunday

THE DAY OF JOY

It was Sunday. I, Cleopas, and my son Simon had been in Jerusalem for the feast of the Passover. Since Friday our minds had been greatly troubled and our hearts sad, for on that day Jesus had been killed.

When Mary Magdalene and some other women had visited the tomb this very morning, they found that the stone had been rolled away and that the body of Jesus was not there. There was no reason for us to stay longer in Jerusalem.

"Let us be going, Simon," I said to my son. "The village of Emmaus is seven long miles from Jerusalem and we want to get there before evening."

As we walked we talked. We could not help thinking about

what Mary Magdalene had told us earlier. A man we did not know joined us and walked along the road with us.

"What are you talking about?" he asked.

Simon and I stood still. Our faces must have shown him our surprise at his question. "You must be the only person who does not know about the events in Jerusalem the past few day," I said.

"What events?" asked the man.

Then we told him the whole story about how Jesus had been crucified. We also told him how the women had found the tomb where Jesus' body had been placed, empty.

"Oh foolish men," said the stranger. "You are slow to believe all the things that have been told you. It was necessary for this to happen to Jesus. Do you not remember how he told his disciples before they entered Jerusalem that he would be delivered to the chief priests, condemned to death, and killed, and that after three days he would arise?"

When we arrived at Emmaus it was evening, so we asked the stranger to stay with us. It was not until we were together at supper that we realized who he was. As we sat at the table he picked up the bread, and blessed it, and broke it, and gave it to us, just as Jesus had always done. Then we knew! This man who had walked with us was Jesus himself!

We hurried to finish our meal so we could get back to Jerusalem. When we found the disciples, they too had good news. "The Lord has risen," they told us, "and has appeared to Simon Peter!" We told them what had happened on the road and as we ate together. Then we knew that Jesus was still with us.

That was a day of great joy for all of us. Jesus was risen, indeed!

PRAYER

O God, our hearts are filled with joy as we think of your great love for us. May we never forget the Easter joy and gladness. Help us always to be true followers of Jesus, our risen Lord. Help us to be faithful members of his church. Amen.